For Amaru,
who was not too small
to make a difference
~ NE

For Luke, Ivy and
Paul
~ SW

MIX
Paper from
responsible sources
FSC® C020056

The Forest Stewardship Council® (FSC®) is an international,
non-governmental organisation dedicated to promoting
responsible management of the world's forests. FSC operates a
system of forest certification and product labelling that
allows consumers to identify wood and wood-based products
from well-managed forests and other controlled sources.

For more information about the FSC,
please visit their website at www.fsc.org

CATERPILLAR BOOKS
An imprint of the Little Tiger Group
www.littletiger.co.uk
1 Coda Studios, 189 Munster Road, London SW6 6AW
First published in Great Britain 2020 • This edition published in 20
Text by Nicola Edwards • Text copyright © Caterpillar Books Ltd 2
Illustrations copyright © Sarah Wilkins 2020
A CIP catalogue record for this book is available from the British Lib
All rights reserved • Printed in China
ISBN: 978-1-83891-1744 • CPB/1800/1658/1120
1 3 5 7 9 10 8 6 4 2

LIKE THE
OCEAN
WE
RISE

LiTTLE TiGER
LONDON

Our planet is vast
and it's beautiful too,

its forests are green
and its oceans are blue.

Do we see that magic and treat it with care?

Do we take for granted the world that we share?

We know that real change
starts with you
and with **me**...

Yet we feel like

raindrops,

small spots on the sea.

But each drop that f$_a$$_l$$_l$$_s$

on smooth water below

makes a **ripple** that echoes, and each one will grow.

In Sweden, one girl said **enough** is **enough**,

it's time to do something, it's time to get **tough**.

She started a ripple.

It grew

and it

grew...

She started us thinking... If not me, then who?

Up here in the Arctic
the shift can be felt.

We can't carry on
letting ancient ice melt.

So we **march** through the snow on the glittery ground.

It's time to take **charge** – we can turn this **around!**

In Queensland, things aren't how we want them to be.
We need to look out for our fish,
for our sea.

Our rainbow-bright coral
is getting bleached white...

Like the ocean, we rise,
and we promise to fight!

In Uganda,
we know that the Earth
is in pain.

We've waited

and

waited

and

waited

for

rain.

Lions and zebras
can't join in our chant,

so we **do**
what the **land**
and the **animals**
can't.

Our magical rainforest's under attack,
our birds and our animals
want their
homes
back.

We won't just stand by

till the **trees**
are all **gone**,

our numbers are **growing** and we will **march on**.

When the rain pours till it feels like a flood,
and we feel overwhelmed, like we're stuck in the mud,

we can help one another, support and protect –
no one is an island, we need to connect.

In Tokyo we fill our
rooftops with **hives**,

we do it to make
sure the honeybee
thrives.

Let's change things
together,

we all have the **power**
to grow bees the gift of a single bright **flower!**

Our skyscrapers here in
New York are so tall,

in the big busy bustle
we're bound to feel small.

But sometimes we just need to open **our hearts,**

when we come together, **that's when** real change **starts.**

As Australia sleeps, Britain's morning begins,
the torch gets passed on as the Earth we share spins.

We pick litter, recycle and keep the seas clean,
we live far apart but we're on the same team.

We **march** here in Delhi
to show that we **care**.

We must use less fuel
so we have cleaner
air.

We're marching, we're singing,

we're banging
the drum...

And we will

not stop until

something is done!

Our planet is vast and it's beautiful too,
but it needs our help – it needs me,
it needs you.

Though we might be small in a world that is wide,
together we swell until
we turn the tide.

What Is Climate Change?

Our planet is getting hotter because more and more harmful 'greenhouse' gases, such as carbon dioxide and methane, are being released into the atmosphere, where they trap heat. We create greenhouse gases when we:

 Burn natural resources (fossil fuels) to power things like transport.

 Cut down trees and use their wood to make products and fuel.

 Raise animals for meat, eggs and dairy, which produces methane gas.

Why does climate change matter?

 As the planet heats, sea ice melts. This destroys habitats for Arctic animals such as polar bears. It also makes sea levels rise, causing floods on land.

 Seasonal patterns change when the planet heats, making it harder for animals to find food and humans to grow crops.

 Extreme weather events such as droughts and hurricanes are also a feature of climate change.

If the planet keeps heating up in this way, it will become harder and harder for humans, animals and plants to survive.

What Can We Do?

 Recycle our rubbish

 Try to buy and use less plastic

Plant flowers (to reduce carbon dioxide and help bees thrive)

Take fewer flights and walk when we don't need to drive

Try to eat less meat and fewer animal products

Get creative and re-use things whenever we can!

We are the future!

In August 2018, 15-year-old Greta Thunberg sat down outside the Swedish houses of parliament with a hand-painted sign and began her 'school strike for climate'. She wanted politicians to tackle climate change and she believed that 'no one is too small to make a difference'.

She was right! Greta inspired a global movement to save the planet. On 15th March 2019, hundreds of thousands of students in more than 2,000 cities around the world protested peacefully in the streets. Hundreds of marches took place as 1.5 million people in over 120 countries stood up for our beautiful planet and its future.

You can help too. You are not too small to make a difference!